The Bears' Bazaar
A Story/Craft Book

written and illustrated by
Michelle Cartlidge

There's going to be a bazaar at Eric and Lucy's school and the little bears need to make something to sell. But what? Mother Bear has some ideas and Father Bear too, and soon the Bear family's house is overflowing with mustard men, moonbirds, and other clever creations.

Young readers will be enchanted by the bears' odds-and-ends transformations as well as Michelle Cartlidge's charmingly detailed watercolor illustrations. As an added bonus, step-by-step directions for all the quick-and-easy crafts are included at the end of the book.

Here's another picture-book gem by the award-winning author-artist of *Pippin and Pod*.

The Bears' Bazaar

A Story/Craft Book

Michelle Cartlidge

Lothrop, Lee & Shepard Books / New York

Eric and Lucy came running out of school to meet their mother with letters in their paws.

"Open them quickly," said Eric.

"We know what's inside," said Lucy excitedly.

Mother Bear read the letters. "There's going to be a bazaar at school," she said. "They want everyone to make things for it. We must think up some good ideas."

When the little bears got home, they raced in to tell their father about the bazaar.

"What are you going to make?" he asked.

"We don't know," said Eric.

"There are all sorts of things you can make from odds and ends around the house," said Mother Bear. "Let's make a list."

"I'll help you make a moving picture show if you like," said Father Bear.

"Can we make mobiles, too?" asked Eric.

"And paper dolls," cried Lucy.

"I'll show you how to make mustard men," said Mother Bear. "And moonbirds. And you can grow spider plants in pots, and make gingerbread bears."

"And surprise boxes!" said Lucy.

"What shall we do first?" asked Eric.

"Why not begin with painted stone paperweights?" said Mother Bear.

So next morning, the bears went out to
find smooth stones of all shapes and sizes.

Father Bear cleaned the stones while the others spread out their ink pots on the table and set to work. At first Eric was in a hurry. He grabbed hold of two brushes at once and sloshed ink everywhere.

"You are messy, Eric," said Lucy.

"I can't do it," moaned Eric, but it wasn't long before he could paint just as well as Lucy. Soon there was a whole row of painted stones on the table— owls, mice, cats, fish. and all kinds of pretty patterns.

"Let's make the surprise boxes next," said Lucy. She brought out all the matchboxes and other tiny boxes she had collected and shared them with Eric.

The little bears made tiny pictures and paper cutouts as the surprises to go inside the boxes. Then they decorated each one gaily on the outside.

"Now we must plant the mustard seeds, so they will be ready in time for the bazaar," said Mother Bear.

She gave Lucy and Eric some empty eggshells. First they drew funny faces on them. Then they filled the shells with earth and sprinkled a few mustard seeds in each one.

"Now we must put them in a dark place for a few days," said Mother Bear, "so the seeds can sprout."

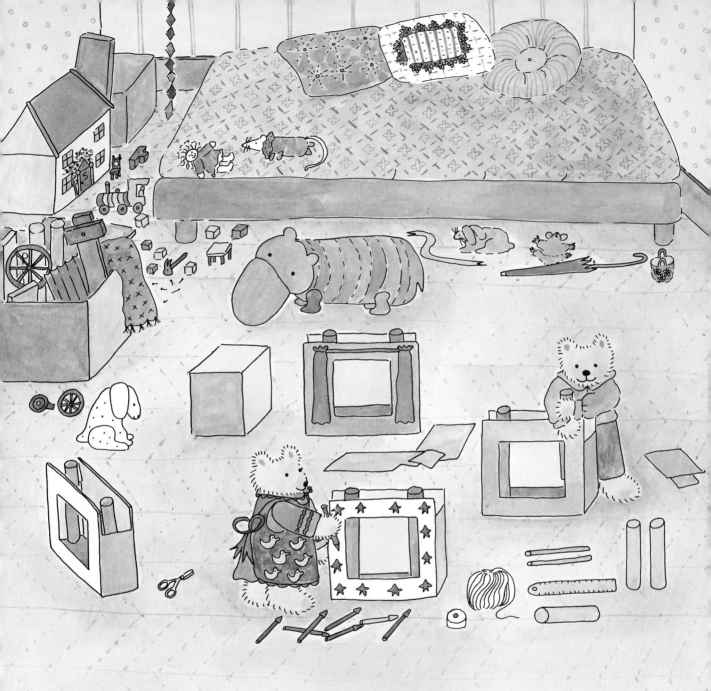

"Why the funny faces?" asked Eric.

"Wait and see," said Mother Bear.

Next day Father Bear showed Eric and Lucy how to make moving picture shows from cardboard boxes. They cut a window in each box and drew stars, stripes, and flowers all over the outside.

Then they made their moving pictures. Lucy drew a cat chasing a mouse. Next she drew a picture of herself looking at the animals in the zoo. Eric drew himself riding a horse, and bears at a fair.

"Let's make the paper dolls next—lots and lots of them," said Eric.

He folded a long strip of paper, and Lucy drew a bear shape on the front. Then they cut around the outline carefully with their scissors. Eric took one end of the paper and Lucy pulled at the other, and a great chain of bears unfolded, all holding paws.

"Let's draw faces on them," said Lucy.

Soon they had hundreds of bears and it was time to make their mobiles.

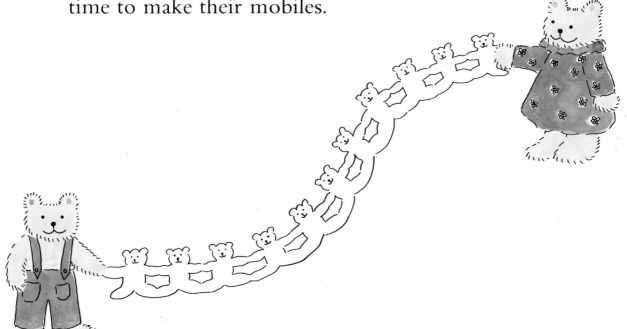

For these, Eric and Lucy drew pictures of mice, foxes, rabbits, squirrels, fish, and birds. They cut them out carefully and painted them on both sides. Father Bear cut pieces of wire and helped Eric and Lucy string their animals up.

Then Father Bear held one mobile while Lucy blew gently to make it turn.

"After the bazaar let's make a mobile for our room," said Eric.

Mother Bear was ready to make the moonbirds.
"I don't know what moonbirds look like," said Eric.
"They live on the moon where bears have never been," said Mother Bear. "So you can invent any bird you like."
The little bears rummaged in the workbox for scraps of leather, cloth, yarn, and fur. Mother Bear showed them how to cut out the body pieces. She sewed the front and back together for Eric and Lucy to stuff.

Then they watched Mother Bear sew all the pieces together—and the first moonbird appeared.

When all the birds were finished, Eric and Lucy set them up around the workbox and made bird noises so Father Bear would come and see their work.

"Such good-looking moonbirds!" said Father Bear.

Eric and Lucy were very pleased.

"I'm going to buy one at the bazaar," said Lucy.

When the bears got up for breakfast the next day, they
noticed that something had happened to their eggshells.
The mustard seeds had sprouted!

"They've got green hair!" said Lucy.

"So that's why we drew faces on the eggshells," said
Eric. "Don't they look funny!"

After school they started the spider plants. Eric carefully picked each little green shoot off Mother Bear's big spider plant. Lucy filled the flowerpots with earth, making sure to put a stone in the bottom of each. Then the little bears planted and watered the green shoots, and put all the pots in a neat row on a shelf.

The afternoon before the
bazaar, Mother Bear mixed her
gingerbread dough. Eric and
Lucy rolled it out and then cut
it into bear shapes.

The smell of the gingerbread bears baking in the oven
made them very hungry.

"Can't we have some now?" begged Eric.

"One each, that's all," said Mother Bear. "Then we'll
put them into bags for the bazaar."

While no one was looking, Lucy quickly stuffed
another gingerbread bear into her mouth. Even Eric
didn't notice. He was too busy arranging all the bags.

Finally the great day arrived. Everyone got up very early. Mother and Father Bear helped Eric and Lucy pack all the things they had made into big bags. They had to be careful that the painted stone paperweights didn't squash the spider plants or the gingerbread bears and that the strings of the mobiles didn't get tangled.

Outside the school there was already a long line of bears. Mother and Father Bear hurried inside to help set everything up. Eric and Lucy had to wait with the others.

"The first thing I'm going to do is look at all the things we've made," said Lucy.

At last the doors were opened. The bazaar had begun!

It was a wonderful bazaar. The little bears stayed to the very end. They couldn't stop talking about it—even when it was time to go to bed.

"Wasn't it fun, Eric?" asked Lucy.

"Yes," said Eric, yawning. "I hope we have another bazaar soon!"

Animal Mobiles

Wire, thin cardboard, nylon or cotton thread, pliers and wire-cutters, scissors, felt pens or paints.

1 Draw animals on the thin cardboard. Cut out and decorate both sides.
2 Lay them out as you want them to hang.
3 Have an adult cut pieces of wire to hang them from (or use a coat hanger), twisting each end of wire into a loop with pliers. Lay the wires above the animals at the height you want the mobile to hang.
4 Find the balancing point of each animal by holding it up. Put thread through each at that point. If the animal does not hang straight, re-thread toward the side pointing downwards.
5 Tie the threads to the wire. Tie another thread to the center of the wire for hanging, moving it back and forth until the mobile balances. You may have to adjust the lengths of wires and threads to make the mobile balance.

Gingerbread Bears

Dough (follow a recipe for gingerbread men, or any rolled cookie recipe), bear-shaped cutters, tiny candy pieces or raisins, crepe paper, ribbons.

1 Roll out the dough and cut it into bear shapes. Make the bear features using the candy or raisins. Bake and let cool.
2 Cut the crepe paper into large circles. Place a few gingerbread bears in the center, gather up around the edges and tie with a ribbon.

Moonbirds

Felt or cloth material, scraps of leather, fur or yarn, buttons for eyes, heavy needle and thread, scissors, leather glue, cardboard, paper, kapok or cotton stuffing.

1 Cut out two oval shapes in felt for the body.
2 Sew together at the edges, leaving a gap at the top for the stuffing.
3 Turn inside out, stuff and sew up the gap.
4 Cut out two circles (leather if you have it, or felt or other material) large enough to form the feet and one slightly smaller circle of cardboard for inside stiffening. Hold the felt circles together with the cardboard circle in the middle and cut out a quarter segment. Keep the segment for the wings. Glue the remainder together to make the feet.
5 Make the beak by cutting two long-sided triangles of leather, one slightly wider at the base. Glue together at the edges, pinching the wider one along the center line.
6 Sew the wings, beak, feet and eyes to the body. Then cover the head with plenty of fur or yarn, sewn or glued on.

Spider Plants

Spider plant cuttings, flowerpots or yogurt containers, stones, soil.

1 Find a spider plant with growing shoots and carefully pick them off.
2 Place a stone in the base of the flowerpot and fill it with soil.
3 Make a hole in the center of the soil, and place one shoot in it. Press the soil firmly around the plant. Water every few days.

Library of Congress Cataloging in Publication Data. Cartledge, Michelle. The Bear's bazaar. SUMMARY: The Bear family spends its free time making different items for the school bazaar. Instructions for their projects are included. 1. Handicraft—Juvenile literature. 2. Cookery—Juvenile literature. [1. Handicraft] I. Title. TT160 C36   745.59   79-13368   ISBN 0-688-41922-4   ISBN 0-688-51922-9 (lib. bdg.)

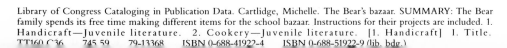

Painted Stone Paperweights

Stones, black felt pen, colored inks, glue-based varnish, paint brush, old brush for varnishing.

1 Wash and dry the stones, then lay them out on newspaper.
2 Draw a design on each with the felt pen and let it dry.
3 With the brush, paint each color separately, letting it dry before starting the next.
4 When the designs are complete and dry, brush them with varnish. Clean the brush in undiluted dishwashing soap.

Surprise Boxes

Matchboxes or other little boxes, self-stick paper in different colors, or colored papers, thin white cardboard, glue.

1 Cut the paper or cardboard to fit snugly inside the box. Draw or paint pictures on it and fit into the box, or make paper cutouts and paste them in.
2 Decorate the outside of the box with self-stick or colored papers.

Mustard Men

Packet of mustard seeds, eggshells, egg cartons, felt pens, soil.

1 Wash and dry the eggshells.
2 Draw funny faces on them, then stand the shells in the egg cartons.
3 Fill each shell with soil. Sprinkle seeds on top of the soil, water, and put the cartons in a dark place.
4 When the seeds start to sprout (from a few hours to a few days later), move the eggshells into the light.

Moving Picture Show

Wooden rod, 2 cardboard rolls, thick cardboard, thin drawing paper, felt pens, cardboard box, cellophane tape, ruler, pencil, saw.

1 Cut a large window in one side of the cardboard box. Decorate around it.
2 Have someone saw two lengths of rod the same height as the box. Cut two equal lengths of the cardboard roll slightly shorter than the rods.
3 Make two holes in the base of the box at either side of the window for the rods to fit into tightly. Tape the rods firmly to the box from underneath and inside. For extra support, cut two cardboard pieces each with a center hole notched outwards to fit tightly over each rod. Slip these over the top of each rod. Then push them down to the base and tape in place to the bottom of the box.
4 Cut or piece together a long strip of thin paper, whose width is a little less than the length of the cardboard rolls. Draw picture shows on it.
5 Tape each end to a cardboard roll.
6 Cut four cardboard discs to fit tightly inside each end of the cardboard rolls. Make a center hole for the rods to go through and place the rolls over the rods.

Paper Dolls

Thin paper, pencil, scissors

1 Cut long strips of thin paper and fold them into accordion pleats.
2 Draw a bear on the top fold, so that all four paws reach the edge of the paper.
3 Cut out the drawing, making sure not to cut through the edges where the paws join.